The Immaculate Chaos of Being

Selected Poems By
Kathleen Wheeler

Kathleen Wheeler

Copyright © 2013 Kathleen Wheeler

All rights reserved.

ISBN: 0615912664
ISBN-13: 978-0615912660 (KatWheelerBooks)

Published by KatWheelerBooks (KWB)
Cover By K. Wheeler
Interior and editing by KWB

This is for you dreamers, you stargazers and mermaids and cloud dancers; you know who you are.

CONTENTS

1	Interlude	1
2	Long Arms to Hold You	3
3	Mind the Cracks	4
4	Endless	5
5	A Dream of Possibility	7
6	The Fates Are Laughing	8
7	Rhythm of a Seacoast Town	9
8	Daily Grind	10
9	Under An Autumn Moon	11
10	Anchor Me	13
11	Impressions of NYC	16
12	The Reinvention of Fire	17
13	Hope For The Butterflies	20
14	Latency	21
15	Drum Break	24
16	Call of the Sea	25
17	How Bold	31
18	Two Hearts Gently Rocking	33
19	Daily Brew	35
20	The Immaculate Chaos of Being	37

Interlude

Fingertips
Sliding
Pressing
Pulling
A song
From
Deep within
The sound
Swirls through
Your body
And sails
Gloriously
From your throat
The music
An exquisite
Melody
Of feeling
Matched
By my own voice
Singing
In harmony
While our
Bodies
Are
Pressed
Together
The vibrations

Felt
In my belly
As we're
Pounding out
A rhythm
A new song
Learned
An old song
Revisited
New melodies
Being written

<u>Long Arms to Hold You</u>

If I could
Reach
Across
The miles
And take
Your pain
Away
I would.
I'd take
Your sickness
And the Soreness
In your
Heart
And the worry
In your soul
And all the
Reasons they
Exist
And leave
Only
The smiles
And the joys
To shine
On...
Even if
Only
For a moment...

I'd do it
In a heartbeat
If I could.

Mind the Cracks

I might
Crack you
Up
From time
To
Time
But I'll try
Very hard
Not to
Shatter
You

Endless

The light
Of a billion
Billion
Stars
Sparkling
In the night
Sky
The moon
Reflecting
On the countless
Dancing
Waves
Of the sea
The nocturnal
Conversation
Between the
Two
A dance
Of light
And love
As one
Mirrors
The other
In an
Endless
Song
Of energy

Just as the
Water
Presses into
The sand
Slowly
Changing its
Shape
So too
Does the
Sand
Hold up
The ocean
And shape the waves
In an endless
Partnership
Of faith
That the
Two will
Forever
Remain
Embraced

A Dream of Possibility

The heart
Feeling
The head
Reeling
The soul
Soaring
The ship
Mooring

The Fates are Laughing

Were we friends
Or lovers
Before our births
And only just
Now
Remember?
Catching
Glimpses
Of a past
In the present
Future
As yet
Unknown
Yet in this
Meeting of
Chance
I am reborn
Once again
Into flesh
Burning
With wonder
At it all

Rhythm of a Seacoast Town

The sounds
Of passing traffic
Cars and trucks
The occasional
Motor home
Children's voices
In laughter
Or cries
People
Young
Old
Asking
Telling
Talking
Shift
In the wind
Breeze of the sea

Daily Grind

the gears
slowly
grind
as gears
grinding
must

the tick tock
of a
ticking
clock

slow
and
slowly
grinding
my bones
to dust....

Under An Autumn Moon

the last fleck of light
fading
the chill
of the breeze
hint of winter
the soft whisper
of the wind
through the trees
as they reach for
that last bit of sun
the song of birds
setting roost
the brilliant hues
of sunset shades
bathing the sky
with their fire
the blackened outline of a
disappearing horizon
the calmness
in our breath
tiny clouds of hope
the awakenings
of life nocturnal
while the day falls
asleep
the chatter
of foraging prey

the near silent swoop
of predator
the electricity
of a touch
the wordless understanding
at a glance
the shrill chorus of crickets
in the distance
sounding out a rhythm
the crunch
and dampness
of grass
the rustling of leaves
the glow
of the moon
as she opens her eyes
to watch her children play

Anchor Me

Forever
Moving
With
The ebb
And flow
Of the tide
Water
Responding
To gravity
The pull
Of the earth
Fighting against
The pull
Of the moon

I'm a leaf
On the breeze
In this life
To see
Where the wind
Will blow me
Seeking
The tree
That would
Hold me
Fast
An anchor

To stay
My flight

As familiar as
Distant memories
Or a child's
Dream
You come
Before me
Already a friend
Cloaked in
A stranger's
Body
I know
You
Yet
So much
Is left
To learn

Tracing
Circles
For paths
I wonder
Have we
Always
Orbited
Thus

And are
Just now
Close enough
To see
Has this
Gravity
Been the anchor
This
Whole
Time?

I need not
The moon
Only the
Light
In your eyes
When
You
See
Me
To keep me
Coming back
To earth

Impressions of NYC

the stench
of garbage
piss
sweat
grease
overripe fruit
pavement
soaks
slithers
and wafts
on the street
in the kitchen
at Burger King
where even the
internet comes
at a price
on the tracks
and tunnel floors
of the subway
dingy

The Reinvention of Fire

Flint
Is a sedimentary thing
Spending time
Building itself
Layer
By layer
Until it has
Substance
And character
Until it is ready
Until it can
Finally
Strike
A bargain
Against the iron
Of resolve
With the
Force
Of two souls
Colliding
Creating a spark
Reflected
In the infinite space
Between the mirrors
Of their eyes
The looking glass
Looking

As they search
For pieces
Of themselves
Within the other
The corresponding
And supplementing
Shapes
The point
And counterpoint
Seeking a tipping point
The equilibrium
Showing a glimpse
Of forever
But only when
The angle
Is just right
The parallel reflections
Reflecting
The ignition
Of a possibility
Of a dream
Of a chance
For something
More
An open door
Or maybe just
A cliff
For freefall

It's all nothing
Without the spark
And the spark
Cannot be
Without the flint
And the iron
And without the spark
The mirrors are simply
Dancing
In the dark

Funny thing about flint…
It has all the time in the world.

Funny thing about iron….
It changes over time.

Funny thing about mirrors….
They can show us what we want to see
And they can show us what's really there;
But only if we look with eyes and hearts open.

And even then, who's to know the difference.

Hope for the Butterflies?

Are you real?
Is the you
You show me
The you
You are?
Or are you
A wolf
Waiting
To make
A tasty morsel
Of my heart?

Latency

Latency is defined as the state of being
Concealed
Or
Not yet made manifest.

It's the delay between
Stimulus and response
An idea and a reality
The space
Between inception
And being what's been conceived...

We're all
Moving
At the speed
Of sound
Sending
Our love
Ahead
To light
The path
Following
Its brilliance
As it reflects
Back to us
From other
Travelers

Travelling
Their own
Courses
Exploring
Their own way
Gamboling
And gambling
The wager
Universal
And we each
Yearn
For the clarity
To see
Where the
Light has
Been
To know
With certainty
That it hasn't been
Swallowed
Up
Or lost
That there's
Someone
Along our route
That's been
Looking
And waiting
For us

To
Finally
Arrive….
There is
No crystal ball
And the light
Has been
Refracted
By all the
Other surfaces
It's bounced off of
To get to you,
But you will
Know me
When you
See
It
And I am
Not far
Behind

Drum Break

the rhythm
of a heart
beating-
the tempo
of a life
living-
a drumbeat
can stand alone
and guide the dance
in solitude
or it can
join the circle
and be made
richer by a
harmonious
melody...

Call of the Sea

Floating
In a sea
Of dreams
Breathless
And bated
I've waited
For what?

The memory of
A whispered
Wordless
Tome
Our history
The ripple
Of the sea
Come
Flooding
Home
From distant
Shores
To wash away
The barriers
That time
Apart
In this life
Has made

To Touch
You
Again
In that
Most deep
And secret
Place
Behind
Your face
Beyond
The flesh
And the
Bone
Again
To touch
You with
My soul's
Embrace…
Pure grace

Where the
Smile in my eyes
Stays
Counting the days
And nights
The ways
And sights
Between
Now

And infinity
Seeking
The promised
Eternity

The reflection
Of the spark
That was you
Long ago
Yet remains
A mark
Like a scar
Of a wound
That will
Never heal
I can feel
You
The vibration
Of a sound wave
The melody of
A long forgotten
Opus
Composed
Of a thousand
Thousand
Thoughts and
Desires
Shared
And fulfilled

Now white noise
The calming
Crashing of
The tide
Lapping
At the sands
Of time
A rhyme

The heart's
Flex
And flexion
Bending to
The construct
Of convention
Separates
When the
The soul
Would venerate
What is
Faith
If not
The belief
In endless
Possibility?
Or at the least
An unlikely
Probability?

The recognition
An admission…
The ticket
A chance
For a dance
Under the stars
The sky is
No greater
Than we
No more
Vast
And here
At last
You see me
And you know
Finally
And definitively

The key
To unlock the
Mystery
Is simply
A look
A caress
To gain access
To the
Parts
Our ourselves
We haven't

Shown
In this life
To relearn
Again
As before
Simply
Open
The door
Connected
Again we threads
In this tapestry
The fabric
Fate wears
When she's being
Modest
The sparks
Reflected
In the mirrors
Of our eyes
The tremor
Of your thighs
No longer
Weighted
But
Breathless
And sated

Floating in a
Sea of dreams

How Bold?

Dare I Be
So bold
Again
And follow
The intuition
Of potential
Love?
Or potential love
Lost?
Do I take
A breath
And take
The leap
Or do
I listen
To the
Pained voice
Of reason?
Knowing that
There is no
Reason
In the realm
Of love
How bold
Do I
Dare
Be?

It would be
So easy
Just
To close
My eyes
And fall....
But I want
To fall
With my eyes
Open
For
You.

<u>Two Hearts Gently Rocking</u>

Two hearts gently rocking
To the beat of their own drum
Two hearts gently rolling
Two loves becoming one…

Two bodies slowly burning
In the fire of their desire
Two souls entwining
Learning to fly ever higher

If you can Rock me Gently
When the World Gets to be
Too much

Rock me Hard
When I'm Aching
For your secret Touch

Rock me Slowly
When I need Some space and
A little time to Breathe

Rock me Solid
Before you Turn to
Leave

Rock me Through the Night

When I need Your softest
Words

Rock me All day long
When I Need to be
Absurd

Rock me as I'm rocking you
And I'll Rock you
In kind and Kindness
All life Long

Two worlds
Rocking Together-
Love is Never Wrong.

Daily Brew

drip drip drip
the coffee drips
into the pot
a dribbling stream of
steamy alertness
the elixir of awake
zombie no more
once i've
filled
my cup

drip drip drip
the coffee drips
into the pot
a dribbling stream of
scalding reality
if the caffeine
doesn't wake you
the burnt tongue will

drip drip drip
the coffee drips
into the pot
a dribbling stream of
consciousness
pulling me out
of my gooey slumber

poor man's prozac

drip drip drip
the coffee drips
into the pot
a dribbling stream of
routine
on second thought,
i'd like some tea

The Immaculate Chaos of Being

doors
close
windows
open
we breathe
in
we breathe
out
sharing
breath
the air
on butterfly
wings
ripples
around
the sphere
of our
existence
tipping dominoes
of actions
and words-
the immaculate
chaos
of being

change
is the

only thing
that
stays
the
same
the delta
of swirling
truth
and half-truth
the perception
of a kiss
of a life
of a death...

chapters
end
credits
roll
yet
the story
is never
truly
over
as one thing
becomes
another
all just
atoms
forming

The Immaculate Chaos of Being

molecules
bouncing
and bounding
like pinballs
in the endless
machine
of a
shared
reality
becoming
matter
and it
matters...
the chemistry
of ideas
multiplied
by the
physics
of feeling

each
one of
us
carries
a light
the
spark
of fathomless
and unquantifiable

depths
it's the
soul
the secret map
on the journey
and it's
written
on the stars
we're
only
just now
relearning
the language...

again.

ABOUT THE AUTHOR

A precocious child, Ms. Wheeler started writing at an early age. Early published work includes poetry and various newspaper articles; more recent work consists of trade papers and marketing content for various clients. While the more technical writings have steered her career path, she never lost her love of writing creatively. In September of 2012, she independently published (through KatWheelerBooks) her first substantial work of fiction, a well received novel titled 'Changing Shape.'

In her spare time, Ms. Wheeler enjoys playing the guitar, painting, cooking, playing with her Wheaten Terrier and getting outside and showing the world to her son.

You can contact Ms. Wheeler through her Facebook profile at www.facebook.com/katwheelerbooks, Twitter @KatWheelerBooks, via email at katwheelerbooks@gmail.com or check out her blog at https://www.katwheelerbooks.blogspot.com

www.ingramcontent.com/pod-product-compliance
Lightning Source LLC
Chambersburg PA
CBHW030306030426
42337CB00012B/612